PHILOSOPHY AND PSYCHOLOGY

THE STUDY OF WISDOM vs THE MOOD OF THE SOUL

To Esther and Isabelle… you girls are so special!

Love,

Dad

Philosophy & Psychology

The Study of Wisdom vs the Mood of the Soul

Chapter 1

Foundations and Divergences

Introduction

Philosophy and psychology are two disciplines that, while often intersecting, have distinct origins, goals, and methodologies. Philosophy, traditionally defined as the "love of wisdom," seeks to bring clarity the fundamental nature of reality, existence, and knowledge. Psychology, on the other hand, is the scientific study of the mind and behavior.

The Origins of Philosophy

Philosophy's roots can be traced back to ancient civilizations, where early thinkers began to question the nature of the world and their place within it. The pre-Socratic philosophers of ancient Greece, such as Thales, Anaximander, and Heraclitus, sought to explain natural phenomena without resorting to mythology. Their inquiries laid the groundwork for subsequent philosophers like Socrates, Plato, and Aristotle, who expanded the scope of philosophical inquiry to include ethics, politics, metaphysics, and epistemology.

Socrates, often regarded as the father of Western philosophy, introduced the Socratic method—a form of dialogue that seeks to uncover underlying beliefs and stimulate critical thinking. Plato, his student, established the Academy and contributed significantly to metaphysical and epistemological discussions, particularly through his theory of forms. Aristotle, Plato's student, developed a comprehensive system of philosophy that encompassed logic, science, ethics, and politics, and his works influenced countless generations of thinkers.

The Emergence of Psychology

Psychology, as a distinct scientific discipline, emerged much later than philosophy. Its roots lie in the philosophical inquiries of figures like René Descartes, John Locke, and David Hume, who pondered the nature of the mind and human experience. However, it was not until the late 19th century that psychology began to establish itself as an empirical science. Wilhelm Wundt, many considered the father of experimental psychology, founded the first psychology laboratory at the University of Leipzig in 1879. His work aimed to investigate the structure of the mind through introspection and experimental methods.

Concurrent with Wundt, William James in the United States was developing functionalism, a school of thought that emphasized the purpose of mental processes in adapting to the environment. Sigmund Freud, with his development of psychoanalysis, explored the unconscious mind and its influence on behavior, introducing concepts like the id, ego, and superego. These foundational figures set the stage for the diverse and multifaceted field that psychology has become today.

Methodological Divergences

One of the primary distinctions between philosophy and psychology lies in their methodologies. Philosophy relies heavily on rational argumentation, critical analysis, and conceptual clarity. Philosophers employ logical reasoning to explore abstract concepts, often without the necessity for empirical verification. This approach allows philosophy to tackle questions that are not easily measurable or observable, such as the nature of justice, the existence of free will, and the meaning of life.

Psychology, in contrast, employs scientific methods to study the mind and behavior. This includes experimental design, statistical analysis, and systematic observation. Psychologists conduct empirical research to test hypotheses and theories, aiming to produce replicable and generalizable findings. This empirical focus enables psychology to make concrete contributions to understanding mental processes, diagnosing mental disorders, and developing therapeutic interventions.

Philosophical Contributions to Psychology

Despite their methodological differences, philosophy has made significant contributions to the development of psychology. Early philosophical debates about the nature of the mind and consciousness laid the groundwork for psychological inquiry. Concepts such as dualism (the idea that mind and body are separate) and materialism (the belief that only physical matter exists) have influenced psychological theories and research.

Moreover, philosophical discussions on ethics have profound implications for psychological practice. The principles of autonomy, beneficence, non-maleficence, and justice guide psychologists in their work with clients, ensuring that their practices adhere to ethical standards. Philosophical reflections on human nature, free will, and personal identity also continue to inform psychological theories and therapeutic approaches.

Psychology's Influence on Philosophy

Conversely, psychology has also impacted philosophy, particularly in areas such as philosophy of mind, epistemology, and ethics. Advances in cognitive science and neuroscience have provided new insights into the nature of consciousness, perception, and decision-making, challenging and refining traditional philosophical positions. Psychological research on cognitive biases, heuristics, and moral development has enriched philosophical discussions on rationality, morality, and human behavior.

The dynamic between philosophy and psychology is evident in contemporary debates on topics such as artificial intelligence, the nature of emotions, and the ethics of mental health interventions. By integrating empirical findings with philosophical analysis, scholars can develop more nuanced and comprehensive understandings of these complex issues.

Philosophy and psychology, while distinct in their origins and methodologies, are deeply measured disciplines that continue to inform and enrich each other. Philosophy's emphasis on wisdom and conceptual clarity provides a crucial foundation for psychological inquiry, while psychology's empirical approach offers valuable insights that challenge and refine philosophical theories. By exploring these fields the human mind and the quest for knowledge and understanding.

Chapter 2

The Nature of Knowledge and Reality

Philosophy and psychology both grapple with fundamental questions about knowledge and reality, but they approach these questions from different perspectives. Philosophy seeks to understand the nature, scope, and limits of human knowledge through epistemology, while psychology investigates how knowledge is acquired, processed, and utilized by the human mind. This chapter explores the epistemological foundations of both disciplines, examining key theories and debates, and highlighting how philosophical and psychological approaches to knowledge and reality intersect and diverge.

Philosophical Perspectives on Knowledge

Rationalism and Empiricism

Philosophers have long debated the sources and nature of knowledge, with rationalism and empiricism representing two primary schools of thought. Rationalists, such as René Descartes, argue that knowledge is primarily derived from reason and innate ideas. Descartes famously declared, "Cogito, ergo sum" ("I think, therefore I am"), emphasizing the certainty of self-awareness and the power of rational deduction in uncovering truths about the world.

Empiricists, such as John Locke and David Hume, contend that knowledge originates from sensory experience. Locke proposed the idea of the mind as a "tabula rasa" (blank slate), suggesting that all knowledge is built from experience and perception. Hume furthered this view by arguing that our understanding of causation and the external world is grounded in habitual associations formed through sensory experiences.

Kantian Synthesis

Immanuel Kant sought to reconcile the rationalist and empiricist perspectives by proposing that while all knowledge begins with experience, not all of it arises from experience. According to Kant, the mind actively shapes and structures sensory input through innate categories and concepts, such as space, time, and causality. This synthesis laid the groundwork for subsequent philosophical discussions on the nature of knowledge and reality, emphasizing the interplay between sensory experience and cognitive structures.

Psychological Approaches to Knowledge

Cognitive Psychology

Cognitive psychology focuses on understanding the mental processes involved in acquiring, processing, and storing information. Key areas of research include perception, memory, problem-solving, and decision-making. Psychologists use experimental methods to investigate how individuals encode, store, and retrieve information, as well as how cognitive biases and heuristics influence reasoning and judgment.

For example, research on memory has revealed the reconstructive nature of recollection, highlighting how memories can be influenced by subsequent experiences and information. Studies on problem-solving have identified various strategies, such as algorithms and heuristics, that individuals use to navigate complex tasks. Cognitive psychology thus provides empirical insights into the mechanisms underlying knowledge acquisition and utilization.

Developmental Psychology

Developmental psychology examines how cognitive abilities and knowledge evolve over the lifespan. Pioneering work by Jean Piaget identified stages of cognitive development, from sensorimotor experiences in infancy to abstract reasoning in adolescence. Piaget's theory emphasizes the active role of the individual in constructing knowledge through interactions with the environment.

More recent research in developmental psychology has explored how social and cultural factors influence cognitive development. Lev Vygotsky, for instance, argued that cognitive development is a socially mediated process, with language and social interaction playing crucial roles in shaping thought processes. This perspective underscores the dynamic and context-dependent nature of knowledge acquisition.

Intersections and Divergences

Perception and Reality

Both philosophy and psychology investigate the relationship between perception and reality, but they do so in different ways. Philosophers ask foundational questions about the nature of perception and the extent to which it can provide us with accurate knowledge of the external world. Phenomenologists, such as Edmund Husserl, emphasize the subjective nature of perception and the intentionality of consciousness, exploring how we experience and interpret phenomena.

Psychologists, on the other hand, study perception through research, examining the neural and cognitive processes involved in interpreting sensory information. Research in visual perception, for example, has uncovered how the brain processes visual stimuli and constructs a coherent representation of the environment. Studies on perceptual illusions and biases reveal the limitations and distortions inherent in our perceptual systems, offering insights into the discrepancies between perception and reality.

Theories of Truth

Philosophical theories of truth, such as correspondence, coherence, and pragmatic theories, address different aspects of how we determine the validity of our beliefs and statements about the world. The correspondence theory asserts that truth is determined by how accurately a statement reflects reality. The coherence theory suggests that truth is a matter of consistency within a set of beliefs. The pragmatic theory, associated with philosophers like William James and John Dewey, posits that truth is determined by the practical consequences of a belief.

Psychological research contributes to these discussions by investigating how individuals assess the truth and validity of information. Studies on cognitive biases, such as confirmation bias and motivated reasoning, reveal how individuals often prioritize information that aligns with their preexisting beliefs and values. Research on the psychology of belief formation and change explores how factors like emotion, social influence, and cognitive dissonance shape our judgments about truth.

Implications for Understanding Human Experience

The interplay between philosophical and psychological approaches to knowledge and reality has profound implications for understanding human experience. Philosophical inquiries provide a conceptual framework for exploring fundamental questions about the nature of knowledge, belief, and reality. Psychological research offers empirical evidence on how these processes operate in practice, highlighting the complexities and nuances of human cognition.

The study of knowledge and reality is a central concern for both philosophy and psychology, each bringing unique perspectives and methodologies to the table. Philosophy offers deep theoretical insights into the nature and limits of knowledge, while psychology provides empirical evidence on the cognitive processes underlying knowledge acquisition and utilization. By examining the intersections and divergences between these disciplines, we gain a richer and more nuanced understanding of the human quest for knowledge and the nature of reality.

Chapter 3

The Nature of the Self

Philosophical Perspectives on the Self

The Question of Identity

Philosophical inquiries into the nature of the self often revolve around the question of personal identity: what makes someone the same person over time despite changes in their experiences, appearance, and circumstances? Several theories have been proposed to address this question.

<u>Substance Dualism</u>: René Descartes posited that the self is a non-material, thinking substance distinct from the body. This Cartesian dualism suggests that personal identity is rooted in the continuity of consciousness and the thinking mind.

<u>Psychological Continuity Theory</u>: John Locke argued that personal identity is based on psychological continuity—specifically, the continuity of memory and consciousness. According to Locke, a person remains the same over time if they can remember past experiences and actions.

Bundle Theory: David Hume challenged the notion of a stable, enduring self, proposing instead that the self is a single unit of perceptions and experiences without an underlying substance. Hume argued that what we call the self is merely a collection of interconnected mental states.

Narrative Identity: More contemporary philosophers, such as Paul Ricoeur, have emphasized the importance of narrative in understanding personal identity. According to this view, individuals construct their identities through the stories they tell about their lives, integrating their past, present, and future into a coherent narrative.

Psychological Approaches to the Self

Self-Concept and Self-Esteem

Psychology examines the self through constructs like self-concept and self-esteem, focusing on how individuals perceive and evaluate themselves.

Self-Concept: Self-concept refers to the cognitive representation of oneself, encompassing beliefs, attributes, and roles. It is shaped by experiences, social interactions, and cultural influences. Researchers study how self-concept develops over time and how it influences behavior and decision-making.

Self-Esteem: Self-esteem is the evaluative aspect of the self-concept, reflecting how individuals feel about themselves. High self-esteem is associated with positive feelings of worth and competence, while low self-esteem can lead to negative self-perceptions and emotional difficulties. Psychological research explores the factors that contribute to self-esteem, such as social comparison, feedback from others, and internalized standards.

The Self in Social Context

Psychologists also study the self in the context of social relationships and group dynamics. Key areas of research include:

Social Identity Theory: Developed by Henri Tajfel and John Turner, social identity theory examines how individuals derive a sense of self from their group memberships. This theory highlights the role of social categorization, identification, and comparison in shaping self-concept and intergroup behavior.

Self-Determination Theory: Edward Deci and Richard Ryan's self-determination theory explores the role of intrinsic and extrinsic motivation in the development of the self. According to this theory, fulfilling basic psychological needs for autonomy, competence, and relatedness fosters a coherent and integrated sense of self.

Intersections and Divergences

Consciousness and Self-Awareness

Both philosophy and psychology grapple with the nature of consciousness and self-awareness, albeit in different ways. Philosophers like Thomas Nagel and David Chalmers explore the "hard problem" of consciousness, questioning how subjective experiences arise from physical processes in the brain. They examine the nature of self-awareness and its implications for personal identity and the mind-body problem.

Psychologists, on the other hand, study consciousness through empirical research on perception, attention, and self-reflection. They investigate the neural and cognitive mechanisms that underlie self-awareness, as well as the developmental trajectory of self-recognition and self-concept. Studies on mirror recognition in infants and animals, for example, provide insights into the emergence of self-awareness.

The Self and Moral Responsibility

Philosophical discussions about the self often intersect with debates on moral responsibility and free will. Philosophers like Immanuel Kant and Jean-Paul Sartre have argued that our sense of self is tied to our capacity for moral agency and autonomous action. Questions about the nature of free will, determinism, and moral accountability are central to these discussions.

Psychological research on moral development, such as Lawrence Kohlberg's stages of moral reasoning and Carol Gilligan's ethics of care, examines how individuals develop a sense of moral self and ethical behavior. Additionally, studies on the psychology of guilt, shame, and empathy provide empirical insights into the emotional and cognitive processes that underpin moral responsibility.

Implications for Understanding Human Experience

The exploration of the self from both philosophical and psychological perspectives offers a richer and more nuanced understanding of human experience. Philosophical theories provide deep insights into the nature of identity, consciousness, and moral agency, while psychological research offers empirical evidence on how these aspects of the self are formed, maintained, and expressed in everyday life.

By integrating philosophical and psychological perspectives, we can better appreciate the complexities of personal identity, the dynamics of self-concept and self-esteem, and the interplay between individual and social dimensions of the self. This interdisciplinary approach enhances our understanding of the human condition and informs practices in areas such as psychotherapy, education, and ethics.

The nature of the self is a multifaceted and deeply intriguing topic that lies at the intersection of philosophy and psychology. Philosophical inquiries into personal identity, consciousness, and moral responsibility provide foundational insights, while psychological research on self-concept, self-esteem, and social identity offers empirical evidence and practical applications.

Chapter 4

Foundations of Morality

Philosophical Perspectives on Morality

Ethical Theories

Philosophers have developed various ethical theories to explain the nature of moral judgments and the principles that guide ethical behavior.

Utilitarianism: Proposed by Jeremy Bentham and John Stuart Mill, utilitarianism is a consequentialist theory that argues the morality of an action is determined by its outcome. The best action is the one that maximizes overall happiness or minimizes suffering. This theory emphasizes the importance of considering the consequences of actions and aiming for the greatest good for the greatest number.

Deontological Ethics: Immanuel Kant's deontological ethics focuses on the inherent morality of actions rather than their consequences. According to Kant, actions are morally right if they are performed out of duty and adhere to universal moral laws, which he formulated as the categorical imperative. This imperative requires individuals to act according to principles that could be universally applied.

Virtue Ethics: Rooted in the works of Aristotle, virtue ethics emphasizes the development of moral character and virtues, such as courage, temperance, and wisdom. This theory suggests that moral behavior arises from cultivating virtuous traits and striving for eudaimonia, or flourishing, through a balanced and virtuous life.

Meta-Ethics

Meta-ethics explores the nature, origins, and meaning of moral concepts. It addresses questions about whether moral values are objective or subjective, and whether they are based on reason, emotion, or social conventions.

Moral Realism vs. Moral Anti-Realism: Moral realists argue that moral values exist independently of human beliefs and emotions, whereas moral anti-realists contend that moral values are contingent on human perspectives and social contexts. This debate examines the objectivity and universality of moral principles.

Emotivism and Prescriptivism: Emotivists, like A.J. Ayer, argue that moral statements express emotional attitudes rather than factual claims, while prescriptivists, like R.M. Hare, suggest that moral statements function as prescriptions for action rather than descriptions of reality.

Psychological Approaches to Morality

Moral Development

Psychologists study how moral values and reasoning develop over time, focusing on the cognitive and social processes involved in moral growth.

Lawrence Kohlberg's Stages of Moral Development: Kohlberg proposed a stage theory of moral development, suggesting that individuals progress through six stages of moral reasoning, grouped into three levels: pre-conventional, conventional, and post-conventional. Each stage represents a more advanced and abstract form of moral reasoning, from basic obedience to universal ethical principles.

Carol Gilligan's Ethics of Care: Gilligan criticized Kohlberg's theory for its emphasis on justice-oriented reasoning, arguing that it overlooked the importance of care and relational ethics, especially in women's moral development. Her ethics of care emphasizes the role of empathy, compassion, and relationships in moral decision-making.

Moral Cognition and Emotion

Psychological research explores the cognitive and emotional processes underlying moral judgments and behavior.

Dual-Process Theories: Dual-process theories of moral cognition propose that moral judgments arise from the interaction of intuitive, emotional responses (System 1) and deliberate, rational reasoning (System 2). Research by Joshua Greene and others has shown that moral dilemmas often elicit quick, affective responses, which can be overridden by more reflective, utilitarian reasoning.

Moral Emotions: Emotions such as guilt, shame, empathy, and disgust play crucial roles in moral behavior. Psychologists study how these emotions influence moral judgments and motivate ethical actions. For instance, empathy can foster prosocial behavior, while guilt can lead to reparative actions following a moral transgression.

Intersections and Divergences

Moral Universality vs. Moral Relativism

The debate between moral universality and moral relativism is a key area where philosophy and psychology intersect. Philosophers debate whether there are universal moral principles that apply across cultures and contexts, while psychologists investigate how cultural and social factors influence moral values and behavior.

Philosophers like Kant and Mill have argued for universal moral principles based on reason and utility, respectively. In contrast, cultural relativists assert that moral values are shaped by cultural norms and practices, and what is considered morally right in one culture may be deemed wrong in another.

Psychological research on moral relativism examines how cultural differences shape moral reasoning and behavior. Studies by Richard Shweder and others have shown that moral values and judgments can vary significantly across cultures, reflecting diverse beliefs about harm, fairness, loyalty, authority, and purity.

The Role of Reason and Emotion in Morality

Both philosophers and psychologists explore the roles of reason and emotion in moral decision-making, though they often emphasize different aspects.

Philosophers such as Kant emphasize the role of reason and rationality in ethical behavior, arguing that moral principles should be derived from logical consistency and universal applicability. In contrast, Hume and other sentimentalists argue that moral judgments are primarily based on emotions and feelings, asserting that reason is a slave to the passions.

Psychological research supports the view that both reason and emotion play crucial roles in morality. Dual-process theories and studies on moral emotions demonstrate that moral judgments are influenced by a combination of intuitive, affective responses and reflective, rational deliberation. This empirical evidence suggests that moral reasoning is a complex interplay of cognitive and emotional processes.

Implications for Ethical Practice

Philosophical and psychological perspectives on morality has significant implications for ethical practice in various fields, including education, therapy, and public policy.

<u>Moral Education</u>: Insights from both disciplines can inform moral education programs, helping to develop curricula that foster moral reasoning, empathy, and ethical behavior. Philosophical theories provide foundational principles, while psychological research offers practical strategies for promoting moral development and prosocial behavior.

<u>Therapy and Counseling</u>: Understanding the psychological processes underlying moral emotions and judgments can enhance therapeutic approaches to addressing moral conflicts, guilt, and shame. Integrating philosophical perspectives on virtue and moral responsibility can also support clients in developing a coherent moral identity and ethical decision-making skills.

<u>Public Policy</u>: The integration of philosophical and psychological insights into moral behavior can inform public policy and social programs aimed at promoting ethical conduct and addressing moral issues such as justice, equality, and human rights. Policymakers can benefit from understanding the cognitive and emotional factors that influence moral behavior and designing interventions that align with moral principles and psychological insights.

The foundations of morality are deeply explored by both philosophy and psychology, each offering unique perspectives and methodologies. Philosophical theories provide profound insights into the nature of ethical principles, moral reasoning, and the foundations of moral judgments. Psychological research, on the other hand, offers empirical evidence on how moral values are formed, how they influence behavior, and the cognitive and emotional processes underlying moral decision-making.

Chapter 5

The Pursuit of Well-Being

Philosophical Perspectives on Well-Being

Eudaimonia and Virtue Ethics

Aristotle's Concept of Eudaimonia: In his Nicomachean Ethics, Aristotle introduces the concept of eudaimonia, often translated as "flourishing" or "the good life." According to Aristotle, eudaimonia is achieved through the cultivation of virtues, which are traits that enable individuals to live in accordance with reason and fulfill their potential. Virtue ethics emphasizes the importance of developing moral and intellectual virtues, such as courage, temperance, and wisdom, to attain a fulfilling and meaningful life.

Contemporary Virtue Ethics: Modern philosophers like Alasdair MacIntyre and Martha Nussbaum have expanded on Aristotle's ideas, arguing that a virtuous life is essential for well-being. Nussbaum's capability approach, for instance, identifies specific capabilities necessary for human flourishing, such as health, education, and political participation. This approach underscores the importance of creating social and institutional conditions that support the development and exercise of these capabilities.

Hedonism and Utilitarianism

<u>Hedonism</u>: Hedonism is the view that pleasure is the highest good and primary motivator of human action. Classical hedonists, such as Epicurus, argue that the pursuit of pleasure and the avoidance of pain are the fundamental principles guiding human behavior. According to this perspective, well-being is achieved by maximizing pleasurable experiences and minimizing suffering.

<u>Utilitarianism</u>: Building on hedonistic principles, utilitarianism is an ethical theory that evaluates actions based on their consequences for overall happiness. Jeremy Bentham and John Stuart Mill argue that the right action is the one that produces the greatest amount of pleasure or the least amount of pain for the greatest number of people. Utilitarianism emphasizes the importance of considering the collective well-being and making decisions that enhance overall happiness.

Psychological Approaches to Well-Being

Positive Psychology

Foundations of Positive Psychology: Positive psychology, pioneered by Martin Seligman and Mihaly Csikszentmihalyi, focuses on the study of positive emotions, strengths, and factors that contribute to human flourishing. This field seeks to understand and promote well-being by identifying and nurturing the qualities that enable individuals and communities to thrive.

PERMA Model: Seligman's PERMA model outlines five key components of well-being: Positive Emotions, Engagement, Relationships, Meaning, and Accomplishment. Research in positive psychology explores how these elements contribute to overall life satisfaction and mental health, and how they can be cultivated through interventions and practices such as gratitude, mindfulness, and goal setting.

The Science of Happiness

<u>Determinants of Happiness</u>: Psychological research identifies several factors that contribute to happiness and well-being, including genetics, personality, social relationships, and life circumstances. Studies suggest that while genetics and personality play significant roles in determining baseline levels of happiness, intentional activities and social connections can significantly enhance well-being.

<u>Subjective Well-Being</u>: Subjective well-being (SWB) refers to individuals' self-reported evaluations of their own happiness and life satisfaction. Research on SWB examines the cognitive and affective components of well-being, exploring how people perceive and experience their lives. Factors such as income, health, and social support are consistently linked to higher levels of SWB.

Intersections and Divergences

The Role of Virtue and Character

Both philosophical and psychological perspectives recognize the importance of virtue and character in the pursuit of well-being. Virtue ethicists argue that developing moral and intellectual virtues is essential for flourishing, while positive psychologists study character strengths and their impact on happiness and life satisfaction.

Philosophical discussions on virtue often focus on the ethical dimensions of character and the role of reason in guiding virtuous behavior. In contrast, psychological research on character strengths, such as the work by Christopher Peterson and Martin Seligman, emphasizes empirical evidence on the benefits of cultivating strengths like kindness, gratitude, and resilience for enhancing well-being.

Hedonic and Eudaimonic Well-Being

Philosophers and psychologists distinguish between hedonic well-being (focused on pleasure and avoidance of pain) and eudaimonic well-being (focused on meaning and self-realization). While hedonism and utilitarianism emphasize the pursuit of pleasure, eudaimonic approaches, both philosophical and psychological, highlight the importance of meaning, purpose, and the actualization of one's potential.

Psychological research supports the idea that eudaimonic activities, such as pursuing meaningful goals and fostering personal growth, contribute to long-term well-being more significantly than hedonic pursuits. Studies show that while pleasurable experiences can enhance momentary happiness, meaningful activities provide deeper and more enduring satisfaction.

Implications for Enhancing Well-Being

Integrating philosophical and psychological perspectives on well-being can inform practical strategies for enhancing individual and collective well-being. By combining the ethical insights of virtue ethics and the empirical findings of positive psychology, we can develop holistic approaches to well-being that address both moral and psychological dimensions.

Education and Personal Development: Educational programs that incorporate character education and positive psychology interventions can promote well-being by fostering virtues, character strengths, and life skills. Teaching practices such as mindfulness, gratitude, and resilience can help individuals develop the capacities necessary for flourishing.

Therapy and Counseling: Therapeutic approaches that integrate philosophical insights on meaning and purpose with psychological techniques for enhancing positive emotions and strengths can support clients in achieving well-being. Practices such as cognitive-behavioral therapy, positive psychology interventions, and existential therapy can be combined to address both emotional and existential aspects of well-being.

<u>Public Policy and Community Well-Being</u>: Policies that promote social and economic conditions conducive to well-being, such as access to education, healthcare, and social support, can enhance collective flourishing. By considering both philosophical principles of justice and empirical evidence on the determinants of happiness, policymakers can design interventions that foster well-being at the societal level.

Chapter 6

The Nature of Emotions

Philosophical Perspectives on Emotions

Theories of Emotions

<u>Cognitive Theories</u>: Philosophers like Martha Nussbaum and Robert Solomon argue that emotions are closely tied to our beliefs, evaluations, and judgments. According to these cognitive theories, emotions are not merely passive experiences but are shaped by our interpretations of the world. For example, feeling anger might involve the judgment that someone has wronged us.

<u>Phenomenological Approaches</u>: Phenomenologists such as Jean-Paul Sartre and Maurice Merleau-Ponty focus on the lived experience of emotions. They explore how emotions are experienced from the first-person perspective and how they shape our perception of the world. Sartre, for instance, considers emotions as ways of apprehending the world that reflect our projects and intentions.

<u>Sentimentalism</u>: Philosophers like David Hume and Adam Smith emphasize the role of emotions in moral judgments. According to sentimentalism, moral values are rooted in human emotions and feelings, rather than in rationality

alone. Hume argued that reason is the "slave of the passions" and that emotions play a crucial role in guiding ethical behavior.

The Ethical Dimensions of Emotions

Virtue Ethics: Within virtue ethics, emotions are considered integral to moral character. Aristotle, for instance, believed that virtues involve appropriate emotional responses and that moral education includes cultivating the right emotions. Emotions like compassion, courage, and temperance are seen as essential components of a virtuous life.

Moral Responsibility and Emotions: Philosophers also explore how emotions relate to moral responsibility. P.F. Strawson's concept of "reactive attitudes" highlights the importance of emotions such as resentment, gratitude, and forgiveness in holding others morally accountable. These emotions are part of the interpersonal practices that underpin moral responsibility.

Psychological Approaches to Emotions

Theories and Models

Basic Emotions Theory: Psychologists such as Paul Ekman propose that there are a set of basic emotions—such as happiness, sadness, anger, fear, surprise, and disgust—that are universal across cultures. These emotions are thought to have evolved to serve adaptive functions and are associated with distinct facial expressions and physiological responses.

Appraisal Theories: Appraisal theories, developed by researchers like Richard Lazarus and Magda Arnold, suggest that emotions arise from the way individuals evaluate or appraise events in relation to their goals and well-being. This perspective emphasizes the cognitive processes involved in experiencing emotions.

Constructivist Approaches: Lisa Feldman Barrett's theory of constructed emotion challenges the notion of basic emotions. She argues that emotions are not hardwired but are constructed by the brain through the interpretation of sensory inputs, past experiences, and contextual information. This approach highlights the variability and complexity of emotional experiences.
Biological and Neurological Foundations

Neurobiology of Emotions: Psychological research examines the brain structures and neural pathways involved in emotional processing. The amygdala, for example, plays a key role in the detection of emotional stimuli and the generation of emotional responses, particularly fear and arousal. The prefrontal cortex is involved in the regulation and modulation of emotions.

Hormones and Neurotransmitters: Studies also explore the role of hormones and neurotransmitters in emotional experiences. Serotonin, dopamine, and oxytocin, for example, are associated with mood regulation, reward, and social bonding. The interplay between these biochemical substances influences emotional states and behaviors.

Intersections and Divergences

Emotion and Reason

Philosophical and psychological perspectives often intersect in the exploration of the relationship between emotion and reason. While some philosophers, like Immanuel Kant, view emotions as potentially interfering with rational decision-making, others, like Hume, see emotions as integral to moral reasoning.

Psychological research supports a more integrated view, suggesting that emotion and reason are interconnected processes. Theories such as Antonio Damasio's somatic marker hypothesis propose that emotions play a crucial role in decision-making by providing valuable information about the potential outcomes of actions.

Emotional Regulation and Well-Being

Both disciplines examine the importance of emotional regulation for well-being. Philosophers like the Stoics advocate for the regulation of emotions to achieve tranquility and resilience. Stoicism teaches techniques such as cognitive reframing and mindfulness to manage emotions and maintain equanimity.

Psychological research explores various strategies for emotional regulation, such as cognitive reappraisal, expressive suppression, and mindfulness-based interventions. Studies show that effective emotional regulation is associated with better mental health, enhanced relationships, and improved overall well-being.

Implications for Understanding Human Experience

Integrating philosophical and psychological perspectives on emotions enriches our understanding of human experience and offers practical insights for enhancing emotional well-being.

Education and Emotional Literacy: Teaching emotional literacy—understanding and managing emotions—can benefit from both philosophical reflections on the ethical dimensions of emotions and psychological research on emotional regulation. Programs that incorporate these perspectives can help individuals develop healthier emotional habits and improve interpersonal relationships.

Therapy and Counseling: Therapeutic approaches that integrate philosophical insights on the nature of emotions with psychological techniques for emotional regulation can provide comprehensive support for clients. Practices such as cognitive-behavioral therapy, which involves reappraising negative thoughts, and existential therapy, which addresses the meaning and significance of emotions, can be combined to address emotional challenges.

Workplace and Organizational Well-Being: Understanding the role of emotions in the workplace can inform practices that enhance employee well-being and productivity. Philosophical insights on ethical leadership and emotional intelligence, combined with psychological research on stress management and positive organizational behavior, can guide the development of healthy and supportive work environments.

Chapter 7

Free Will and Determinism

The debate over free will and determinism is one of the most profound and long-standing discussions in both philosophy and psychology. It revolves around the extent to which human beings have control over their actions and decisions. Philosophers analyze the conceptual foundations and implications of free will, while psychologists investigate the cognitive and neural mechanisms underlying decision-making and voluntary behavior. This chapter explores the philosophical and psychological perspectives on free will and determinism, highlighting key theories, research findings, and the intersections between these disciplines.

Philosophical Perspectives on Free Will

Theories of Free Will

Libertarianism: Libertarian philosophers argue that free will is incompatible with determinism. They claim that for individuals to have free will, they must have the ability to choose otherwise in a given situation. This view posits that human actions are not entirely determined by prior states of the world or natural laws. Notable libertarians include Robert Kane and Peter van Inwagen, who argue for a form of agent-causal libertarianism, where agents themselves are the originators of their actions.

Compatibilism: Compatibilists maintain that free will can coexist with determinism. They argue that free will does not require absolute freedom from causation but rather the ability to act according to one's own motivations and desires. Classical compatibilists like David Hume and contemporary philosophers like Daniel Dennett suggest that free will is about acting in accordance with one's internal states, even if those states are determined by prior causes.

Hard Determinism: Hard determinists argue that free will is an illusion because every event, including human actions, is determined by preceding events and natural laws. Philosophers like Baron d'Holbach and Galen Strawson argue that because our choices are determined by factors beyond our control, we cannot be truly free. This perspective emphasizes the implications of determinism for moral responsibility and ethical behavior.

Moral Responsibility

The question of moral responsibility is deeply intertwined with the free will debate. If our actions are determined, can we be held morally responsible for them?

Libertarianism and Moral Responsibility: Libertarians argue that free will is necessary for moral responsibility. If individuals have genuine control over their actions, they can be praised or blamed for their behavior. Without free will, concepts like guilt, punishment, and reward would lose their meaning.

Compatibilism and Moral Responsibility: Compatibilists assert that moral responsibility is compatible with determinism. They argue that as long as individuals act in accordance with their desires and intentions, they can be held accountable for their actions. Compatibility theories often focus on the importance of rational deliberation and voluntary control in attributing moral responsibility.

<u>Hard Determinism and Moral Responsibility</u>: Hard determinists face the challenge of explaining moral responsibility without free will. Some, like Derk Pereboom, suggest that we should revise our understanding of moral responsibility and adopt practices that emphasize rehabilitation and social harmony rather than punishment and blame.

Psychological Approaches to Free Will

Cognitive and Neuroscience Research

Decision-Making Processes: Psychological research explores the cognitive processes involved in decision-making, examining how individuals perceive options, weigh alternatives, and make choices. Studies on bounded rationality, pioneered by Herbert Simon, reveal that human decision-making is often constrained by cognitive limitations and environmental factors.

Neuroscientific Studies: Neuroscientific research investigates the brain mechanisms underlying voluntary actions and decision-making. Benjamin Libet's famous experiments on readiness potential suggest that unconscious neural processes precede conscious awareness of decisions, challenging traditional notions of free will. More recent studies by researchers like Patrick Haggard and John-Dylan Haynes continue to explore the neural correlates of voluntary action and the implications for free will.

The Illusion of Free Will

<u>Automaticity and Unconscious Processes</u>: Psychological research highlights the role of automatic and unconscious processes in behavior. Studies by John Bargh and others show that many of our actions are influenced by automatic responses to environmental stimuli, suggesting that conscious control may be more limited than we perceive.

<u>The Sense of Agency</u>: The sense of agency refers to the subjective experience of controlling one's actions. Research in cognitive psychology explores how this sense is constructed and how it can be influenced by various factors, such as timing, feedback, and context. Findings suggest that the feeling of free will may be, at least in part, an illusion constructed by the brain.

Intersections and Divergences

The Concept of Agency

Both philosophical and psychological perspectives examine the concept of agency, though they often emphasize different aspects.

Philosophical Agency: Philosophers focus on the conditions necessary for genuine agency, such as intentionality, rational deliberation, and the ability to act otherwise. They explore the implications of different theories of free will for our understanding of human autonomy and moral responsibility.

Psychological Agency: Psychologists study the mechanisms underlying the experience of agency, investigating how people perceive control over their actions and the factors that influence this perception. They explore how agency is constructed in the brain and how it affects behavior and decision-making.

Determinism and Human Behavior

The debate over determinism intersects with psychological research on the predictability of human behavior.

Philosophical Determinism: Philosophers analyze the implications of determinism for concepts like freedom, responsibility, and ethical behavior. They explore whether determinism undermines the notion of human agency and how it affects our understanding of moral responsibility.

Psychological Predictability: Psychologists study the extent to which human behavior can be predicted based on prior states and environmental factors. Research on behavioral genetics, environmental influences, and cognitive biases reveals the complex interplay of factors that shape human behavior, suggesting that while behavior can be influenced by prior conditions, it is not entirely predictable.

Implications for Human Understanding and Practice

Integrating philosophical and psychological perspectives on free will and determinism offers valuable insights for various aspects of human life, from ethics and law to mental health and personal development.

Ethics and Law: Understanding the interplay between free will and determinism can inform ethical theories and legal practices. For example, legal systems that recognize the influence of determinism on behavior might focus more on rehabilitation than punishment, emphasizing social and psychological support for offenders.

Mental Health and Therapy: Exploring the concepts of agency and control can enhance therapeutic practices. Therapists can help clients understand the factors influencing their behavior and develop strategies for increasing their sense of agency and making more intentional choices. Cognitive-behavioral approaches, which emphasize the role of thoughts and beliefs in shaping behavior, can benefit from integrating insights on free will and determinism.

<u>Personal Development</u>: Understanding the balance between determinism and free will can empower individuals to take responsibility for their actions while acknowledging the influences beyond their control. This balanced perspective can promote personal growth, resilience, and ethical behavior.

The debate over free will and determinism is a central concern in both philosophy and psychology, offering rich insights into the nature of human agency, moral responsibility, and decision-making. Philosophical theories provide deep reflections on the conceptual and ethical dimensions of free will, while psychological research offers empirical evidence on the cognitive and neural mechanisms underlying voluntary behavior.

Chapter 8

The Meaning of Life

Philosophical Perspectives on the Meaning of Life

Theories of Meaning

<u>Existentialism</u>: Existentialist philosophers like Jean-Paul Sartre and Albert Camus emphasize the individual's role in creating meaning in an inherently meaningless world. According to existentialism, life has no intrinsic meaning, and it is up to each person to construct their own purpose through their choices and actions. Sartre famously declared that "existence precedes essence," underscoring the idea that humans are free to define their own essence.

<u>Absurdism</u>: Albert Camus' philosophy of absurdism highlights the tension between humans' search for meaning and the indifferent universe. In "The Myth of Sisyphus," Camus describes the absurd hero who, despite the lack of inherent meaning, continues to strive and create meaning through their actions. Camus suggests that one must embrace the absurdity of life and live with passion and integrity.

Nihilism: Nihilism, associated with philosophers like Friedrich Nietzsche, posits that life lacks inherent meaning, value, or purpose. Nietzsche's concept of the "will to power" offers a response to nihilism, suggesting that individuals can create their own values and meaning through their actions and creativity. Nihilism challenges traditional sources of meaning and calls for a reevaluation of life's purpose.

Sources of Meaning

Theistic Perspectives: Many philosophical traditions find meaning in life through religious or spiritual beliefs. Theistic perspectives assert that life has purpose and value derived from a divine source. Philosophers like Søren Kierkegaard and Thomas Aquinas argue that faith in God provides a foundation for meaning and guides moral and ethical behavior.

Humanism and Secularism: Humanist and secular philosophies find meaning in human experiences, relationships, and achievements. Thinkers like Bertrand Russell and Martha Nussbaum emphasize the importance of human flourishing, social justice, and the pursuit of knowledge and creativity.

Secular humanism advocates for creating meaning through compassion, reason, and the betterment of humanity.

Psychological Approaches to the Meaning of Life

Theories and Models

Frankl's Logotherapy: Viktor Frankl, a Holocaust survivor and psychiatrist, developed logotherapy, a form of existential therapy that focuses on finding meaning in life, even in the face of suffering. In "Man's Search for Meaning," Frankl argues that the primary drive in humans is the "will to meaning." He suggests that individuals can find meaning through work, relationships, and adopting attitudes that transform suffering into a source of growth.

Self-Determination Theory: Edward Deci and Richard Ryan's self-determination theory (SDT) posits that humans have basic psychological needs for autonomy, competence, and relatedness. According to SDT, fulfilling these needs contributes to a sense of meaning and well-being. Research within this framework explores how intrinsic motivation and personal growth enhance life's meaning.

Positive Psychology: Positive psychology, pioneered by Martin Seligman and Mihaly Csikszentmihalyi, investigates the factors that contribute to a meaningful and fulfilling life. Seligman's PERMA model (Positive Emotion, Engagement, Relationships, Meaning, Accomplishment) identifies meaning as a key component of well-being. Positive psychology emphasizes the importance of finding purpose through personal strengths, goals, and social connections.

Research on Meaning in Life

Sources of Meaning: Psychological research identifies various sources of meaning in life, including relationships, work, spirituality, and personal growth. Studies show that having meaningful goals, engaging in prosocial behavior, and cultivating a sense of purpose are associated with higher life satisfaction and mental health.

The Benefits of Meaning: Research indicates that a sense of meaning in life is linked to numerous positive outcomes, such as increased happiness, resilience, and overall well-being. Meaningful living is also associated with better physical health and longevity. Studies suggest that finding meaning can buffer against the negative effects of stress and adversity.

Intersections and Divergences

The Construction of Meaning

Both philosophical and psychological perspectives explore how individuals construct meaning in their lives.

Philosophical Construction: Philosophers examine the existential and ethical dimensions of meaning construction. Existentialists, for example, argue that meaning is created through authentic choices and actions. Humanist philosophers emphasize the role of reason, creativity, and social engagement in building a meaningful life.

Psychological Construction: Psychologists investigate the cognitive and emotional processes involved in meaning-making. Research explores how individuals interpret life events, set goals, and find purpose through personal narratives and social connections. Theories like narrative identity suggest that people create meaning by integrating their life experiences into coherent and purposeful stories.

Meaning and Suffering

Both disciplines address the relationship between meaning and suffering.

Philosophical Perspectives: Philosophers like Nietzsche and Camus discuss how confronting and overcoming suffering can contribute to a deeper sense of meaning. Nietzsche's concept of "amor fati" (love of fate) encourages embracing life's challenges as essential to personal growth and meaning. Camus' absurd hero finds meaning through the defiant struggle against life's inherent absurdity.

Psychological Perspectives: Psychological research, particularly in positive psychology and logotherapy, examines how individuals find meaning in the face of suffering. Studies show that people can derive meaning from adversity by reinterpreting their experiences, focusing on personal growth, and engaging in altruistic behavior. Resilience and post-traumatic growth are often linked to the ability to find meaning in difficult circumstances.

Implications for Enhancing Meaning in Life

Integrating philosophical and psychological perspectives on the meaning of life can inform practical strategies for enhancing individual and collective well-being.

<u>Education and Personal Development</u>: Educational programs that incorporate philosophical reflections on meaning and psychological research on well-being can help individuals develop a deeper sense of purpose. Teaching practices such as critical thinking, ethical reasoning, and goal setting can foster personal growth and meaningful living.

<u>Therapy and Counseling</u>: Therapeutic approaches that integrate existential and positive psychology can support clients in finding meaning and purpose. Practices such as narrative therapy, logotherapy, and strengths-based interventions can help individuals navigate life's challenges and build meaningful lives.

<u>Community and Social Engagement</u>: Promoting meaning in life at the community level involves creating opportunities for social connection, civic engagement, and cultural participation. Policies and programs that support education, mental health, and social justice can enhance collective well-being and provide individuals with a sense of purpose and belonging.

Chapter 9

The Nature of Consciousness

Theories of Consciousness

Dualism: Dualism, most famously advocated by René Descartes, posits that the mind and body are distinct substances. According to Cartesian dualism, the mind is a non-physical entity that interacts with the physical brain. This view raises questions about how mental and physical states interact and the nature of subjective experience.

Physicalism: Physicalism, or materialism, asserts that everything about consciousness can be explained in terms of physical processes. Philosophers like Daniel Dennett and Paul Churchland argue that consciousness arises from brain activity and can be fully understood through neuroscience. Physicalism faces challenges in explaining subjective experiences, known as the "hard problem of consciousness."

Panpsychism: Panpsychism is the view that consciousness is a fundamental feature of the universe, present even in the smallest particles. Philosophers like David Chalmers and Philip Goff propose that consciousness might be a basic aspect of reality, like space and time. Panpsychism offers an alternative to dualism and physicalism by suggesting that all matter has some form of consciousness.

Idealism: Idealism posits that reality is fundamentally mental or immaterial. Philosophers such as George Berkeley argue that the external world is a construct of our minds and that physical objects only exist insofar as they are perceived. Idealism raises questions about the nature of perception and the relationship between mind and reality.

The Hard Problem of Consciousness

Qualia: Qualia refer to the subjective, qualitative aspects of conscious experience, such as the redness of red or the pain of a headache. The challenge of explaining qualia is central to the hard problem of consciousness, a term coined by David Chalmers. Philosophers debate whether qualia can be fully accounted for by physical processes or if they point to a non-physical aspect of the mind.

Intentionality: Intentionality is the capacity of the mind to be directed toward objects, states, or concepts. Philosophers like Franz Brentano and John Searle explore how mental states can represent or be about something.

Understanding intentionality is crucial for explaining how thoughts and perceptions relate to the external world.

Phenomenal Consciousness vs. Access Consciousness: Ned Block distinguishes between phenomenal consciousness, which involves the subjective experience of being aware, and access consciousness, which refers to the cognitive processes that enable information to be accessible for reasoning and behavior. This distinction highlights the complexity of consciousness and the challenges in developing a comprehensive theory.

Psychological Approaches to Consciousness

Cognitive and Neuroscientific Research

Neural Correlates of Consciousness (NCC): Neuroscientists investigate the brain structures and processes associated with conscious experience. Research identifies regions such as the prefrontal cortex and the thalamus as crucial for various aspects of consciousness. Studies using techniques like fMRI and EEG explore how brain activity correlates with conscious states.

Global Workspace Theory: Bernard Baars' global workspace theory suggests that consciousness arises from the integration of information across different brain regions. According to this theory, a "global workspace" acts as a hub for information processing, making certain information available for conscious access and cognitive control.

Integrated Information Theory (IIT): Giulio Tononi's integrated information theory posits that consciousness corresponds to the capacity of a system to integrate information. IIT provides a mathematical framework for measuring the complexity of conscious states and suggests that higher levels of integrated information correspond to more vivid and differentiated experiences.

Altered States of Consciousness

Sleep and Dreams: Psychological research explores the nature of consciousness during sleep and dreaming. Studies on REM and non-REM sleep reveal different patterns of brain activity associated with various stages of sleep. Dreams provide insights into the workings of the unconscious mind and the functions of memory and emotion.

Meditation and Mindfulness: Practices like meditation and mindfulness can alter states of consciousness and provide insights into the nature of awareness. Research shows that meditation can enhance attention, emotional regulation, and well-being. Studies on the neural effects of meditation reveal changes in brain regions associated with self-awareness and cognitive control.

Psychedelics: Psychedelic substances like LSD and psilocybin induced altered states of consciousness perprotrated by changes in perception, thought, and emotion. Research on psychedelics examines their potential therapeutic benefits and the neural mechanisms underlying their effects. Studies suggest that psychedelics can increase neural connectivity and promote psychological insights.

Intersections and Divergences

Consciousness and Self

Both philosophical and psychological perspectives explore the relationship between consciousness and the self.

<u>Philosophical Perspectives on the Self</u>: Philosophers debate the nature of the self and its relationship to consciousness. Some, like Derek Parfit, argue that the self is a construct without a fixed essence, while others, like Thomas Metzinger, propose that the self is an illusion created by the brain. These debates raise questions about personal identity, continuity, and the nature of subjective experience.

<u>Psychological Perspectives on the Self</u>: Psychologists study the development and functioning of the self, investigating how self-concept, self-esteem, and self-awareness influence behavior and mental health. Research on the self includes studies on autobiographical memory, identity formation, and the impact of social and cultural factors on self-perception.

The Unconscious Mind

Both disciplines address the role of the unconscious mind in shaping conscious experience and behavior.

<u>Philosophical Perspectives on the Unconscious</u>: Philosophers like Sigmund Freud and Carl Jung explore the influence of unconscious processes on conscious thought and behavior. Freud's psychoanalytic theory posits that unconscious desires and conflicts shape our actions and mental states. Jung's concept of the collective unconscious suggests that shared archetypes influence individual consciousness.

<u>Psychological Perspectives on the Unconscious</u>: Psychological research investigates the mechanisms of unconscious processing and its impact on behavior. Studies on implicit memory, automaticity, and priming reveal how much of our cognition and behavior is influenced by unconscious factors. Research on the unconscious mind explores the interplay between conscious and unconscious processes in shaping perception, decision-making, and action.

Implications for Understanding Human Experience

Integrating philosophical and psychological perspectives on consciousness can enhance our understanding of human experience and inform practical applications in various fields.

Mental Health and Therapy: Understanding the nature of consciousness and its disorders can inform therapeutic practices. Approaches such as mindfulness-based therapy, psychoanalysis, and cognitive-behavioral therapy can benefit from insights into the conscious and unconscious processes that influence mental health. Therapeutic interventions can help individuals develop greater self-awareness, emotional regulation, and well-being.

Artificial Intelligence and Machine Consciousness: The study of consciousness has implications for the development of artificial intelligence and the possibility of machine consciousness. Philosophical and psychological insights into the nature of awareness, intentionality, and subjective experience can guide the creation of more sophisticated and ethical AI systems. Questions about the potential for machine consciousness and its moral status challenge our understanding of what it means to be conscious.

<u>Ethics and Society</u>: Exploring consciousness raises ethical questions about the treatment of conscious beings, including animals and potentially conscious machines. Philosophical and psychological perspectives can inform debates on animal rights, personhood, and the ethical implications of creating conscious AI. Understanding the nature of consciousness can also guide ethical decision-making in areas such as medicine, law, and social policy.

Made in the USA
Columbia, SC
12 July 2024

ae7303a2-05b6-4799-90de-d5cd9fc7236fR01